AF322662

Waging War On The Night

Waging War On The Night

Jacob Z. Waldroup

IngramSpark

Contents

Contents

Contents

Contents

{ ix }

Contents

To all who have made this possible
Thank you,
J.

{ 1 }

Waging War On The Night

As she descends down on us cloaking all light with her veil.
Her one and only mission? To make life a living hell.

The night satan's mistress attacks within our minds.
She and her army bleed dry all they can find.

No one is safe from her, she's always close by.
Never are we out of sight from her all seeing eye.

When we're at our lowest that's her favorite time.
To sink her teeth into us like a grape straight from the vine.

She doesn't play fair in her attacks on the mind.
She holds us each a prisoner of war.
Freedom from her grasp is what we're fighting for.

Waging war on the night is the only way.
To restore the light within ourselves to once again be whole.
Until the night strikes again, peace within our soul.

{ 2 }

A Time When

There are times of love, times of laughter.
Times when a shove is all we need.
In order to excel, in order to succeed.

No matter which path you traverse in life.
You're going to meet joy, you're going to meet strife.

Sometimes it all comes down to a time when.
Were given a choice to keep going, or begin again.

We can choose to stay down, we can choose to fight.
Each day like a battle, waging war on the night.

All Black

Out in the darkness under the cover of night.
No way to reach out, no means of sight.

The world around you draped by a dark shroud.
No star in the sky, not even one cloud.

No way to know which way you're going.
Dressed in all black, no part of you showing.

A sound in the distance causing your heart to race.
Was anyone looking for you, can you keep up the pace?

You're traveling, to get out from under afar.
Trying to make it out of the battle, without as much as a scar.

All Those Around

If it weren't for all those around.
I would remain lost, never to be found.

If it weren't for the ones who are there.
The ones who show kindness, the ones who show care.

If it weren't for those who mean the most.
Would I have given up, would you be reading this post?

You see for me it was all those around.
Who kept me safe, who kept me sound.

If it weren't for each of them playing a part.
In standing beside me, in shielding my heart.

In each of the battles waging war on the night.
They were my strength, my reason to fight.

Alone Again (Tonight)

Here I am alone again tonight.
With nothing to accomplish, no reason to fight.

Deep within this jungle, the mess that's in my head.
Do you see me, did you hear what I said?

Here I am alone again tonight.
No reason to get up, no ending in sight.

As I sit and watch the sun fade.
I feel myself sinking deeper into the shade.

Allowing the darkness, the shadows of the night.
To win this battle, to win this fight.

Although we may want to, we can't win them all.
Sometimes we need that someone to catch us when we fall...

{ 6 }

Are You Too?

The way I've felt more commonly these days.
As if there's no feeling, trapped within the maze.

That is my mind.
Tell me where will I find.

A way out of here.
Tell me, tell me my dear.

Is there an option to get out of here?
Should I tread with extreme caution?
Is there reason to fear?

Tell me is there a way out of this labyrinth In my mind?
Tell me is peace out there for me to find?

Tell me you're feeling what I'm feeling too.
Tell me dear friend, are you too?

Before You Go

Walking down a path you've traveled so many times.
Now covered by vines.

Grown up with no care.
Unsure exactly how you ended up there.

It had been a while since you'd walked this road.
Turning to leave, you hear faintly behind a voice saying.

Before you go leaving this place.
Please know it was never meant to be a disgrace.
Life can be cruel in so many ways.
This path is an example of the toll.
It can take on our mind, body, and soul.
Take this with you as you go.

The stranger then handed you a rose.
So fragrant it tickled your nose.

Then added the best part of all.

Although there are tolls, we all have to pay.

JACOB Z. WALDROUP

There's always a bright spot in every day.

You see, this rose was grown,
from the madness that once was a path.
Long overgrown by life's wrath.
Beauty can rise from the ashes before our eyes.
We just have to remember to look.

Believe

Some say there's a light which comes from within.
Each one has a purpose, a reason to defend.

Tell me my darling, is this what you believe?
Is it my light you're hoping to receive?

Is that why you've brought me here?
Away from my safe space to a place which brought fear.

Is this your way of helping me get through?
This state of being that turned my light blue.

Tell me my darling, is this what you believe?
Was this your mission that you hope to achieve?

{ 9 }

Bleeding Slowly (Words That Can Hurt)

Many don't realize we each conceal.
A weapon within us bound by our seal.

Many don't realize the power within.
The way words can hurt, even the closest of friend.

Many don't realize we each can cause.
Another to bleed slowly, due to our failure to pause.

You see the tongue, sharper than any knife.
It holds the power over another's life.

It's all it tasks to stain their shirt.
They're now bleeding slowly, from words that can hurt.

Come Sit With Me (By The Light Of The Moon)

We all may be waging our own war on the night.
No one ever said we had to do it alone though, right?

Come sit with me by the light of the moon.
Don't worry there's always plenty of room.

For any of you to come sit anytime.
No need to bring anything yourself will be fine.

No matter the burden your soul must bear.
No matter the hour I'll always be there.

So come sit with me by the light of the moon.
Don't worry it'll be over all too soon.

Dark Side (Of the Soul)

We all have one whether we show it or not.
A dark side of the soul tied together in a knot.

Some present it sweet with a bow.
Striking from behind like a viper on a doe.

Their innocent victim never saw it coming.
If they had would they have started running?

Away from the venom in your fangs.
Injecting the darkness deep into their veins.

Turning their blood cold as ice.
Wasn't she a good girl, wasn't she nice?

What happened to her, they'll never know.
She let the dark side of her soul show.

Destruction of the Night

Explosions crashing into the night.
Blinded by flashes taken out on site.

No where to run, nowhere to hide.
Was this how you imagined the end would come?

If only you could get up, if only you could run.
Yet you're lying there in a sea of carnage.

Watching the battle happening all around.
Sinking deeper into the ground.

The night was winning as your thoughts descend.
No way to fight, no way to defend.

Within yourself a war is fought.
The destruction of the night, the goal which is sought.

Coming out of hiding at the first sight.
The breaking of dawn casting out a great light.

The war is over, the battle fought.

The destruction of the night has come to pass.
Yet your beating heart, still fragile as glass.

Different (Yet Still The Same)

We're all different, yet still the same.
Each our own player within the game.

Set out with objectives to achieve.
Our faith in another is why we believe.

We can do this, come whatever may.
We can fight the night seeing another day.

We all have something we face alone.
Within our minds, our souls home.

We may all be different, yet still the same.
Lean on one another to get through to the end.
What is life without a friend?

{ 14 }

Does It Feel The Same?

Tell me my darling, how does it feel?
To finally have each, and every thrill.

Which you ever dared to dream.
No matter the extent of your latest scheme.

Tell me my darling, how does it feel?
Does it feel the same, is this actually real?

Can you look in the mirror as you walk out the door?
Tell me my darling what was it all for?

Now that you have it is it all that you need?
Alone in your castle, only your name on the deed.

Tell me my darling are you happy now?
With the crowd snarling hoping you go down by the bow.

Tell me my darling was it worth it all?
No matter how fast you fall.

Cast out from the graces of what once was your home.

Tell me my darling, how's it feel being alone?

Does It Make It Worse?

The war on the night comes creeping in.
When it's least expected it has the power to send.

Your mind jumping from the tallest of them.
Into the depths of your soul again.

Does it make it worse to let anyone in?
Showing a weakness, beginning again.

Can bring a low point seen as a disadvantage.
Tell me you see you still have chances.

To make a change within yourself.
Coming out of your shell, placing your fears on a shelf.

Tell me you see the the power within.
The strength you hold, standing up with the best of them.

Don't Give Up (Don't Give In)

You thought no one saw the struggle you bore.
You hid it well beneath the floor.

Bottles half empty searching for more.
Panic stricken you couldn't be sure.
That you would make it past a quarter till four.

All the while knowing you're not off work until five.
You sit there and wonder how you're even alive.

Periods of time you can't remember.
Relationships burnt out, not even an ember.

Remains with a single someone.
Tell me dear friend, did you have more fun?

Then you realized, the cost of the game.
Now you feel it, you'll never be the same.

It went from a glass to calm you at night.
To bottles on bottles keeping you alive.

Funny when the one thing keeping you going.
Is the same as what's killing you from within.

Tell me, was it worth it to drink your poison?
I know that you can do this, you're stronger than them.

Please don't give up, don't give in.
I know you can do this; you have it within you to win.

{ 17 }

Don't Say (You Understand)

Bridges burning all around.
Yet no one is screaming, not even a sound.

Can they not see it, as the flames grow higher.
Can they not feel it, the snapping of wires.

Tell me how no one is reacting.
Is this scene something exactly.

The reason, like all of them before.
The weight that I carry, the slamming of doors.

The distance between continues to vary.
Unless you've been there, right where I am.
Please don't say you understand.

{ **18** }

Don't Worry (I Got You)

Worry not my love.
I'm with you here fit like a glove.

No need to fear as I'm by your side.
No longer a need to run and hide.

Your aura such a vibrant hue, scaring away anything in the dark.
The light cast from within creating a spark.

Which can defend against all that come your way.
Bringing forth color casting out the gray.

That was there throughout the night.
It was always within you, the will to fight.

You only needed to see who you are, and who you can be.
Don't worry I got you, trust me you'll see.

No matter what comes remember to have fun.
Your light from within shines bright like the sun.

Drunk on the Night

Some need the sun to fuel their lives.
Others need the moon to just get by.

Living In a world filled with crisis.
Yet here we are leaning on our vices.

Tell me my darling, can't you see?
Nothing in this world comes for free.

Feeling numb, ignoring the pain.
Comes at a price becoming the bane.

Of our existence in every way.
Each and every single day.

Tell me my dear, are you willing to pay?
The price it takes to stay.

Drunk on the night, no feeling again.
Barely existing, wallowing in the nights den.

Of self loathing, pity, and shame.

Tell me is the price worth it to escape the pain?

{ 20 }

Excuses (For the Pain)

No we don't always say what we feel.
Making excuses for the pain as if it's not real.

Our castles crumbling all around.
Lost beneath the rubble to never be found.

Dreams lost, hopes shattered.
As if any of it even mattered.

When you're young they lead you to believe.
In happy endings we're meant to achieve.

A picture painted in black and white.
Not one drop of color anywhere in sight.

With lines that are clearly drawn.
Tell me the difference between right and wrong.
If we cross them were we bad all along?

In a world where we're shamed for feeling.
Sending even the strongest head reeling.

Hurrying to come up with the latest excuse.
To avoid the pain detouring the noose.

We make excuses for the pain.
So that we blend in looking somewhat sane.

Then again by who's definition.
Should we be silenced into submission?

As members of culture.
Why are we picked off by each our own vulture?

Like something stalking its prey in the night.
Refusing to lay down giving up the fight.

To live in a world where it's wrong to feel.
That isn't a world I accept to be real.

{ 21 }

Find Someone (Their Hope Is Fading)

Find someone their hope is fading.
How much longer can they go on degrading.

Their mind, body, and soul.
Raking themselves across the coals.

Allowing society to take away their variety.
By placing over them the veil of the night.
Blocking out the sun, taking away all light.

Find someone their hope is fading.
Their will to fight is further jading.

Each day just a bit more.
In every way as the ones before.

Isn't there someone out there who cares?
To stay by their side, to see how they fair.

Isn't there one? That's all it takes.

To reintroduce the sun, burning all the snakes.

With its rays of warmth and light.
I'll be damned if I lose another friend to the night.

Finding the Light

Like an eclipse upon our lives.
The sun is blocked out no matter the strives.

That we make to better ourselves real or fake.

It doesn't matter, not anymore.
We bruise and batter keeping our hearts sore.

Forever lurking around in the dark.
Deeply searching for just one spark.

Of creative inspiration finding the light we've been searching for.
It was always within us behind our hearts door.

Forever Young (Gone Too Soon)

In the midst of war not every battle is won.
Some souls are lost, forever young.

Gone too soon, taken by the nights hand.
Fallen on her sword, removed from this land.

You never know who's at war in their mind.
It's our job to reach out, seeking to find.

The light, covered by her veil.
Saving another from a lifetime of hell.

Not every soldier who takes up arms.
Returns home to the cities and farms.

Which they left, at least in the same state.
As casualties of war, we're altered by the night.
Each uniquely haunted by what they saw.

Some left behind, forever young gone too soon.

Waging War On The Night

Light a candle as the clock strikes noon.

In honor of a lost soul.
Bringing them home safely is always the goal.

{ 24 }

Fucked Up (Faded)

Although once a shiny new toy.
I now rely on a need to be coy.

On the outside I'm strong as steel.
When on the inside it doesn't feel real.

Some say I'm fucked up, even faded.
To them I say they're clearly jaded.

No matter how kind I seem to be.
They always find a reason to leave me.

Standing here alone in the dark.
Reaching out for even one spark.

Of ignition to continue to hope.
After so long now how can I continue to cope?

Maybe they're right, I've faded away.
If I weren't here, then what would they say?

Tell me why they all must ghost.

Waging War On The Night

Am I really that bad of a host?

Is my company done so in vain?
Am I so fucked up that nothing's the same?

For me, as it is for them.
If only I weren't me, perhaps if I were him.

Then they would like me and be willing to stay.
Yet if I weren't me then who would pay?

The price of their sick little joke?
Someone come save me before I stoke.

Up the fire within my heart.
Come now my darling, come be a part.

{ 25 }

Haunted

We'd all be lying if we didn't admit.
There are things from our past which cause us to sit.

There and shake, chilled to the bone.
What was that name there on that headstone?

Jacob something, from 1910.
No this can't be happening again.

Forever haunted by the ghost of my past.
Tell me how long this one will last.

Unsure if I have the strength to defend.
Isn't there someone you can send?

To reassure me, calming me down.
Someone please help me get the hell out of town.

There's no way I can continue this path.
As long as I'm haunted, I'm cursed by his wrath.

It's up to me to break this cycle.

Waging War On The Night

I'm no longer afraid to say his name, Michael.

The thing that happened between him and I.
That's long over now, an eye for an eye.

Like the old saying even at last.
I'm leaving it all there, tucked away in the past.

Now I'm not haunted, not anymore.
All I had to do was leave closed that door.

Haven't Had

In the dark my heart awakens.
Yearning for the one for my love to partake in.

It's been a while now.
Since I've seen the warmth of your smile how.

Can I keep going without you here?
It's been so long since you've been near.

I haven't had, not even one friend of that kind.
Since our loves end it's you, I can't get off my mind.

I sit and wonder by the moons light.
Should I have given up, did I put up enough fight?

For the one that my heart called home.
With it the sun shaded by stone.

Now sits firmly in the sky.
Why did I let this be our goodbye...

Here In The Dark
(Without You)

Cold November, no one around.
The fires gone out, not even a sound.

Within our house can be heard.
To think of it empty is simply absurd.

As I'm here in the dark without you again.
Waging war in my heart that'll never end.

It's been forever since you left.
Taking with you the light in the theft.

Of my house, you were the robber.
I didn't have it in me to try and stop her.

From taking what was mine.
A life we'd built, swinging from vines.

That were the obstacles in our minds.
Which together we would overcome.

Now I'm here in the dark without you again.
Tell me my darling, am I being punished for some sin?

How Much Time (Is Left On The Clock?)

Whispers making their way around town.
Not one yet knowing of the blood-soaked gown.

Which I saw that night.
Running, screaming with no sound coming out.

My voice failing from the fear.
Tell me my darling, tell me my dear.

How much time is left on the clock?
Ticking above you, which one day will stop.

In your dreams you see it clear.
Haunted by time, a ghost we all fear.

Tell me do you see it, near or far?
Does it distract you, wherever you are?

Hurt

On a boat you sit and wonder.
Will the pain you hide behind that smile.
Continue to hurt, leading to exile.

Motor roaring in your ears.
You barely hear it, overthinking your fears.

Your mind going mad, like a ripple in a pond.
Was it your fault, you felt they were fond.

Of you and all you could bring to the table.
They didn't see it though, you would never be able.

To escape the hurt in your mind.
Using whatever excuse you could find.

To escape any situation as the fear came creeping in.
You knew it was over, time to begin again.

As you let the hurt from your past.
Keep anything good in your life from being able to last.

{ 30 }

I Can Hear You (But I'm Somewhere Else)

What? I'm sorry I'm miles away.
No worries, that's okay.

I was just saying, the fellow began.
When my mind drifted away once more.
Hello are you listening? Slamming shut my minds door.

You seem so far away.
The look in your eyes, are you okay?

I'm sorry I can hear you, but I'm somewhere else.
My mind seems to insist I not be myself.

With you for more than a moment.
Why I'm unsure, there isn't much on it.

It seems there's something my body's trying to say.
It feels like there's something more to this day.

Unable to put my finger on it I say.

Is there any chance you know of anything happening today?
Something I should be aware of before it slips away.

Not that I know of. The man exclaimed.
That's when it hit you, intensely with pain.
Right in the gut remembering their name.

A name you hadn't allowed even your mind to think.
Remembering now the reason your ship sank.

Today was the day when you close all the curtains.
Todays the day you're silent, this you're certain.

Todays the day you turn off the phone.
Not answering the door, pretending no one is home.

Todays the day when it went down.
The day they let your heart drown.

Although you can hear them, you're somewhere else.
Remembering now you've forgotten the reason.

Faintly reminded you're over it now.
Ship no longer sinking by the bow.

Heart no longer full of regret.
No longer a need to fret.

You've come this far, to not even recall the day.
Perhaps next year you won't remember at all.
Allowing the memories to fade like the leaves in the fall.

{ **31** }

I Don't Need (Anyone Else)

The sun shining in.
Through my window again.

Leaving the depths of my unconscious mind.
Back into reality is where I find.

Myself, once more.
Desperately seeking to close the door.

Hiding away.
Unable to seek out the rest of the day.

Yet I know that isn't what I'll do.
I don't need anyone else, not even you.

To make it through this day.
I'll rise from the ashes painting on a smile.
Perhaps it'll become real, that hasn't happened in a while.

Knowing it to be unlikely, for now this will do.
I don't need anyone else, not even you.

I have myself, I'll make it through.
Single handily changing the tint of this hue.

Tomorrow will come, the sun rising once more.
Isn't this what we're all fighting for?

I Don't Need (That Much)

Some have plenty, some have none.
Some take from others, that's fun.

For me though, I don't need that much to get by.
As long as I've got a dream in my heart, and a gleam in my eye.

My needs I handle with utmost care.
Making sure they're always there.

Food on the table, clothes on my back.
There's little in life I seem to lack.

Thankfully able to provide for my life.
What so many can't manage without strife.

Yet I do fine, the way I am.
I don't need that much, I do what I can.

I Let Myself Down Today

Monday through Friday no different than another.
Wake, work, eat, sleep, repeat.

Waiting until Saturday just to rest.
How did I end up here, did I fail some test?

In life, exhaustion as the punishment for my crime.
Was I meant to suffer every time?

Sleeping over half the day away.
Groggily rising to ignore the list of chores.

That had been put off throughout the week.
Was this what I wanted; was this the life I seek?

Continually finding myself disappointed.
I let myself down today.

Realizing I was the cause for some of my pain.
If only I'd do better, I'd learn how to gain.

All the things I'm missing as the days in my life go by.

Waging War On The Night

Perhaps if I were a blue jay I could learn to fly.
No longer being responsible for either you or I.

Letting go of the chains which have held me down.
Finally, my turn to sing a happy song.

Instead of complaining with another day of waste.
Tell me why when we were young, we dreamed of making haste.

To these days where we thought we'd be free.
Yet it turned out this way.

If only we knew then, what we know now.
Wondering what could have been if we'd taken our time.

Enjoying those days each a bit more.
Instead, we're looking back wondering what the hells this all for?

So little makes sense.
Unless you're in that one percent.

If you're here on the bottom like most of us are.
It's not easy to make it very far.

Without help of some kind.
These are the things I can't get off my mind.

Anyway, I let myself down today.
Here's to hoping tomorrow is better.
For now, I sit here writing this letter.

Addressed from me to the fire.
Maybe one day I'll fulfill my heart's desire.

{ 34 }

I Made It Through

As the light fades away slowly, a little at a time.
Suddenly I'm no longer feeling fine.

A chill washing over with the shadow of the night.
Covering In her darkness everything in sight.

Unable to see as I rise from the chair.
Imagining the room, right there's a table there.
Moving a bit out of the way seeing how I'd fair.

I make my way through the maze.
Navigating the room in this dark daze

If you'd only known the steps I've taken.
I made it through the darkest days.
Days I can't even share with you.

I care not to recall the battle which was fought.
Nothings fair in war, this is what I was taught.

Firsthand as my castle came crumbing down.
Around me with no one in sight, nor one sound.

In my ears as my body had gone into shock.
I didn't realize then I'd been pelted by a rock.

Of deceit causing my blood to paint the wall.
As the towers behind me continued to fall.

Most of my safe place gone, only rubble in its wake.
This is war after all, send in the troops already for my sake.

{ **35** }

I Need You (Better)

You think no one can see?
I see.
You think no one can hear?
I hear.
You haven't been well in a while my dear.

You let on as if you're okay.
Hoping those around you will stay.

If they ever knew.
You fear would they leave you?

Unable to imagine a life alone.
Yet every time you give into your vice.
You're as alone as the darkness of night.

Unbeknownst to another, or so you thought.
Can I help you not think about those thoughts?

I need you better, so you can know.
A life without vices, confined by devices is possible.

I need you better, I need you okay.
What will I tell the world, what will I say?

If anything were to happen to you.
I don't think I could ever, tell me who.

Would I have to help me through the night.
When I need a laugh, or a therapy session with a friend.
Who would I go to? Who would I spend my life confiding in?

If you were gone, I would spend the rest of my life searching.
For another to feel the void.

I need you better, so you can be okay.
So you can be happy living out fully your days.

I need you better, so that you can see the world around.
I know you have it in you, I know the strength can be found.

You have me to lean on, in any time of need.
I need you better, I need you here with me.

I Need You (To Tell Me)

Walking in on you again.
To find us where we began.

Sitting there, a stranger in our home.
Never have I felt more alone.

Sometimes I just need you to tell me that you care.
That you're still there.

I need you to tell me you'd do anything to stay.
To help us grow, to keep things this way.

Would be to keep a rose from the light.
Eventually it withers losing one petal at a time.

Until it's barren, like the wasteland that has become my heart.
I need you to tell me before I start.

To give up on us all together.
Forgetting what mattered, unable to see forever.

With you as the one by my side.

Waging War On The Night

No longer needing to try any longer.

What good would it do?
If only you'd tell me, then I would know it's always been you.

I've given my heart to.
It was always you, that got me through.

All the times up late at night.
Unable to sleep, unable to fight,

Alone without your help.
There wouldn't be a reason to be here today.

I need you to tell me so that I know.
That what my heart fears is not so.

I Remember

Bunker shaking with each blast.
I sit here alone now afraid to ask.

How near is the end? Unable to cry.
The memories flooding back, in this ditch I lie.

A soldier at war only twenty-one.
I'm not ready to go, my lives just begun.

There's so much left I want to see, want to do.
The only thing now getting me through.
Is the memory of us, which I'll come home to.

How I remember the look on your face.
When I gave you that rose on our first date.

The look in your eyes the day I finally kissed you behind that tree.
The way you leaned in as if you'd been longing to kiss me.

It was always you.
The one who got me through.

Waging War On The Night

All the days waging war on the night.
I will continue to fight.

To get back to you and our home.
I will not be consumed, another casualty reduced to bone.

In a pile, soul no longer there.
Don't worry baby, I will find a way back.
Surviving the battle with nothing but this sack.

Which holds my belongings, the little I'm able to carry.
If I make it out of here, would you want to marry.

Me, after all this time?
Is it too late now? I haven't a dime.

Only myself I have to give.
The skin on my back, the will to live.

And love making a great life.
If I make it out of here, a survivor of the war on the night.

{ 38 }

I Should Be (But I'm Not)

Six am being woken again.
Everyday for the last thirty one years.

Off to a job which I love, or once did.
I know I should be happy, but I'm not.

You see I'm a teacher.
Long overworked, long underpaid.

Gone are the days where children were raised with respect.

These children get wilder as the years go by.
Some days after work, I sit in my car and just cry.

Emotionally exhausted unsure how I'll make it through another
day.
It's more than I can bare now, something I never thought I'd say.

I've wanted this life as long as I can remember.
Anytime anyone asked, it was never a question.
What do you want to be? A Teacher.

Waging War On The Night

Not understanding the burden which came.
There's no compensation that could begin to measure.
The emotional war we face each day.

As hundreds of lives are in our care.
As so many children pass through every year.

We who do it, do so out of love.
If it weren't for that, and a bit of help from above.

There's no way we would make it through another year.
Some of these children even instill fear.

Into our hearts, with their lack of empathy.
It's our job to better our youth for tomorrow's generation.

The care provided a great collaboration of minds, hearts, and
souls.
Coming together as one becoming our goal.

I Won't Forget

I won't forget, where I came from.
I won't forget, the days without sun.

I won't forget, the pain which came.
I won't forget, drowning in the rain.

I won't forget, the sting of the night.
I won't forget, the burn of time as it passes me by so slow.
I won't forget, the moon and her glow.

I won't forget, the way you came.
Pulling me out of the darkness, drenched from the rain.

I won't forget, you nursing my wounds.
I won't forget, staying up with you until noon.

I won't forget, when the sun came out.
I won't forget, who was there during the drought.

{ 40 }

If I'm Being Honest

If I'm being honest, I'd tell you the truth.
Could you handle it? If I show you the proof...

If I'm being honest, I'd show you the scars.
The marks on my heart, while I was trapped behind bars.

Captured a prisoner of war.
A war of the heart, which I didn't sign up for.

You see I was drafted against my will.
Dragged out of my home screaming, carried down the hill.

To the truck, thrown in the back.
Could they not see, the courage I lack?

If I'm being honest, the pain that came.
Was worse than any I'd know again.

If I'm being honest, I don't know how I'm here.
Living each day in hell and fear.

If I'm being honest, I didn't think I would make it this far.

Is that understood?

If I'm being honest, the scars that I bare.
Now battle scars I proudly wear.

If I'm being honest, I made it through a war of the heart.
Something I saw coming from the start.

Yet I ignored, like so many others.
A war which is fought between lovers.

A war which no one ever really wins.
Each leaving the other worse off than they began.

Some being able to survive this war.
Those are the ones who realize what the fights for.

Energy isn't put into something without care.
If they didn't, they wouldn't be there.

Fighting in the midst of the storm.
On the battlefield hearts worn.

If they didn't, do you think they'd be torn?
At all, from the stumble, the fall.

Of the battle, the one which was fought.
Hopefully the lesson to each has been taught.

{ 41 }

In The Last Days (A Story Would Unfold)

In the last days, a story would unfold.
Events transpired; a life was stolen.

In the last days, before the storm.
A family was lost, their home once warm.

In the last days, they couldn't have known.
The strength it would take to overcome that which had grown.

In the last days, the air began to chill.
In the last days, one of us would seal.

The fate of the life we knew.
In the last days, the rumors that flew.

Telling our story, yet were they true?
As in the last days no one knew.

Exactly how it happened, or what went down.
The only half remaining had long fled town.

The whispers grew deep into the night.
As in the last days we lost our sight.

On what was truly there.
Losing a union found to be rare.

Two as one, a love so strong.
Yet in the last days each were wrong.

Neither could see past the edge of deceit.
Neither able to find Their feet.

As both ran, one would stumble leading to both their fall.
In the last days, they would lose it all.

{ 42 }

In The Last Days (Of My Life)

Middle of winter, bitter is the night.
With nothing around me, no shelter in sight.

Cast out here alone again.
Heart grown cold from within.

Betrayed by the ones who meant the most.
Those I would fight for from coast to coast.

Yet here I am in the last days of my life as I know it.
Traversing this maze, everything changed.

In the blink of an eye.
No will left within me, no emotions left to cry.

No desire to stay, no reason to die.
Looking up not seeing a single star in the sky.

Nor a cloud in sight.
As the battle raged on in the war on the night.

43

In The Last Days (With You Here)

In the last days with you here.
I held you close, you were always near.

Never far from my touch.
Brushing off the rust.

That had grown between our hearts.
Through distance and time, each playing our parts.

In the battle which was fought.
In the war on the night, you won, I lost.

The aftermath is where it bloomed.
I couldn't see past the gloom.

Which was growing within my mind.
Without you here I couldn't find.

A reason to get out of bed.
Constantly fighting this war in my head.

Which is what lead us here.
Now you're the one consumed by fear.

I didn't mean to take it that far.
In the last days before the fire.

I just needed some kind of escape.
I didn't plan for this to happen.

Trust me, I never imagined we would be here.
These last days, hold me now as I continue to pay.

The price for my own actions.
As I become our personal faction...

44

It's Hard (Trust Me I know)

It's hard, trust me I know.
I've been there unable to go.

Anywhere without bombs crashing down.
Around me without a sound.

I run, I scream, I cry.
I fall to my knees looking up at the sky.
Begging God to tell me why.

Although I know there's a will in his plan.
It's still hard to be here taking the stand.

It's never easy being a casualty of war.
Especially when you don't know what it's all for.

It's hard, trust me I know.
Once over you'll have scars proudly to show.

Telling the story of where you've been.
Telling the story of the battle you were in.

It's the only way in life to grow.

{ **45** }

It's Not (Worth It)

Middle of May enjoying the breeze.
Spring sprung around you, new growth of the leaves in the trees.

Which tower over all, casting shade upon everything below.
Protecting it from the sun allowing it to grow.
Without feeling the burn, a happy medium no need for concern.

Trust me it's not worth it, to throw yourself on the fire.
No matter how strong your heart may desire.

Trust me it's not worth it to give your all.
To something, or someone who doesn't care if you fall.

Trust me it's not worth it to carry that load.
A burden you bore protecting the code.

Of your heart when the enemy was already within.
Trust me it's not worth it to fear the need to begin again.

Do not fear what will bring you joy.
Even though it's hard, you're nothing more than a toy.

Waging War On The Night

For them, you've seen it yourself.
Obsessed at first, then tired and on a shelf.

When the new wears off.
Trust me it's not worth it to take this loss.

Sometimes in war, especially of the heart.
We have to remind ourselves before we can start.

Sometimes in battle our hearts can unravel.
Making us second guess our decisions.
Perhaps we can save them, even making it better.

Trust me it's not worth it to sacrifice your self worth.
To cater to some jerk who will never give birth.

To your happiness, allowing your true self to shine.
Trust me it's not worth it to give up our peace of mind.

{ 46 }

It's Not (Your Fault)

Oh my darling come now sit by the fire.
Don't blame yourself for your hearts desire.

You see the heart is a fickle little thing.
With joy also comes pain.

Trust me my darling it isn't your fault.
There's no need to worry, no need to be distraught.

Trust me my darling I've got your back.
There's nothing we can't handle that's a fact.

Trust me my darling it not your fault.
At no time in battle can ones heart be bought.
Only the love therein can be sought.

By another thusly given to.
Trust me my darling it's not your fault that you're blue.

Unfortunately we can't win every battle of war.
As long as we make it out, sometimes that's all we hope for.

Waging War On The Night

Trust me my darling you're safe with me now.
Lie your head on my shoulder as I tell you how.

It's not your fault, there's no need to cry.
There will always be plenty of other guys.

Trust me my darling, it's not your fault.
Within you is a lion which can't be caught.

Up in battle as it reigns over all.
King of the many, protector from our hearts fall.

Trust me my darling it's not your fault.
You're going to make it through this, I'll be by your side.
With you always until the day that I die.

Then beyond as I watch over you from afar.
Sending you light, just look up into the stars.

There I am, can you feel my warmth?
Trust me my darling it's not your fault.
See I'm with you always even in the dark.

It's Okay To Feel (All The Things)

Hello, can I help you on your way?
I'm sorry I'm not from around here,
it seems I've lost much of the day.

No worries, I assure you I know the way well.
Go ahead and brush yourself off, I can see that you fell.

Come sit at my table, rest awhile.
I'll make you a meal while you warm by the fire.

Tell me dear traveler what brings you this way?
It is unfortunate you lost much of the day.

I'm on my way to start anew.
I've left a life once lonely and blue.

As you should I assure you so.
Many loads in life we carry, no matter which row we hoe.

Rocky are the hills we climb, some steep and narrow,

taking many bumps and bruises along the way.
Fighting an emotional war of the heart
can turn anyone's world gray.

I'm here today to tell you it's okay,
to feel all the things that come your way.
It's the victories in battle, the scars that we bare,
to be proud of as they help us grow.

Without pain in life, we wouldn't enjoy the good that comes.
Take the rainbow for example.

Such beauty that came from a storm.
We never know in life which way our hearts will form.

Some are lucky and have little they have to pay.
Then those who aren't as much, who have to fight every day.

Either way your life goes just take this with you and know.
It's okay to feel all the things it's what helps you grow.
Through the pain.

Lost In The Liquor

Going out with your friends, leaving me here alone again.
What are you doing? It's only four p.m.

Getting wasted on a Tuesday night.
Are you serious, are you looking to fight?

You have work in the morning.
If you get fired we'll lose it all.

I can't carry this load without you.
I can't do this on my own.

Do you even care?
Seemingly more clear than ever you're lost in the liquor.

Crippled by poisons touch.
How did we get here, when did this become a crutch?

That you have to have to make it through the day.
When did all the color collide becoming gray?

Tell me did you start sinking deeper into this vice.

Waging War On The Night

The more you started drinking to forget about that night.

The night you can't speak of, the night you lost it all.
The night your sanity ran away
as you were pressed against that wall.

I'm so sorry baby, that I wasn't there.
If I had, I would have said take me hands up in the air.

Maybe they would have spared you.
Maybe it was all I had to do.

Yet I wasn't there.
I had said I wasn't feeling well, even though I was feeling fair.

I assured you that I'd be okay.
Love you as you leave, I say.

How was I supposed to know that would be the day,
that I lost you forever to this vice.
I never imagined a day this would happen to our life.

I can't change what happened, I can only help you through.
Now you're lost in the liquor, the result of what happened to you.

How can I help you? Tell me what I can do.
Please help me change your world,
back from gray to that vibrant hue.

That we loved, your smile, your, warmth, your laugh.
Please help me to help you, there has to be some way back.

Tell me what you need baby, I love you, I say.

As I walk out the door off to another day.

Of work leaving you there alone.
Praying the entire shift that you'd be okay,
when I arrived back home.

How do you help someone who's given up all hope?
How do you help someone who lost,
not just a battle, but the entire war.
How can you explain to them that's what you're there for...

Make This Stop

Make this stop, you say.
Hands in your hair overwhelmed by the day.

Doesn't anyone care? You think as you keep pushing on.
Your flame burnt out, not a song in your heart, not even one.

Although you know many, as you love to sing.
If only singing could buy you a ring.

To place on your finger, to show you were the one,
who made it out of all your peers.
If only you could say that, if only they were here.

Yet no one's here, not anymore.
Long gone are the days you once looked for.

Make this stop, you say again.
Make this stop, these thoughts in my head.
Make my heart come alive, now that it feels dead.

Make this stop, starting my pulse again.
Make this stop, come be my friend.

Lay by me as we look at the stars.
Forgetting this world, and who we are.

Make this stop, for just a moment.
As the war of the night continues to rage on.
Make this stop, tell me you've been here all along.

In the distance just out of sight.
Make this stop, the war on the night.

{ 50 }

Manic Midnights

Twelve chimes of the clock, striking midnight again.
Sneaking up on me like an old friend.

Here I am sitting by the fire.
Burning nearly as hot as my heart's desire.

To create from within.
A burning passion bore from sin.

Was it greed which drove me here?
To a place where the dawn, I fear.

Or was this just another manic midnight once again.
My mind racing, no rational chasing a high which from me expels.

Into trouble, not a care in the world.
No thought of tomorrow, no thought of today.
Only this moment matters I say.

As I continue on my latest hyper fixation.
Whatever it was that night, whichever creation.

Which I'd put my energy into.
Some bore fruit, as some were thrown into the trash.

With all the others, never seeing the light of day.
Another failure here it comes.

The sun peaking over the tops of the trees which surround.
Another dawn with no glory to be found.

Another failed attempt at becoming something.
Another dawn being nothing.

Manic Midnights take over our minds.
Leading us to a world which ourselves we find.

Is it ourselves? I stop and wonder.
Perhaps just a version that lies dormant within.
Until the clock strikes midnight again.

51

Meet Me Under the Bleeding Stars

Meet me under the bleeding stars.
Looking up at the sky burning like fire.

Stars bright red, shining scarlet in the night.
Signaling the battle we're in for a fight.

Body consumed, enthralled by panic.
Why here, why now? I can't help but wonder.

As all my airways are constricted, the room beginning to spin.
Will my life ever be the same again?

Or is this my new reality?
Something I have to learn how to be.

A person who panics fighting within.
To do something as simple as going out with a friend.

Anxiety, a general for the night.
Leading its minions into battle as the war rages on.

Tell me is there hope out there for me to lean on?

So, I ask for you to meet me under the bleeding stars.
When the panic sets in the world becomes far.

From sight, out of mind.
No rational anywhere I can find.

Meet me there, help me through.
Tell me when, tell me who.

52

Melody Of The Night

As the darkness sinks over the land.
Impossible to see, finding a place to stand.

The sun has fallen, replaced by the moon.
What once was bright, now pale with delight.

Casting deep shadows, creating shapes that aren't there.
Tricking our minds getting lost our fair share.

Imagining the things creating the shapes.
What it might be determining our fate.

Perhaps some creature lingering out of sight.
Waiting on us singing the melody of the night.

Attracting us closer with it's sweet sound.
Waiting to pounce once we come around.

Will you run, or pause to take a second glance?
Would you give in, if given the chance?

It's a difficult task finding the courage to keep on the right path.

JACOB Z. WALDROUP

No matter whatever is waiting out there.

We each have to decide whether to rise up and fight.
Or run away taking flight.

Which we choose determining our fate.
If you make the wrong choice will you still end up at the gate?

Which you were always meant to be.
Or will you be lost somewhere in the trees...

53

Midday Dreaming

Forty eight hours a cease fire was called.
Forty eight hours with nothing to report.
Who knew forty eight hours could be so short?

Two small days, the pressures off.
Two large days, spent aloft.

Doing as we each saw fit.
Most spending their days in their civilian outfit.

Yet for me I enjoy peace.
Midday dreaming of the days that were.

Unsure of what life will look like after the war.
However, for forty eight hours our hearts aren't sore.

With the loss of another friend.
To the war on the night as it began again.

So many casualties unable to defend,
against the thoughts in their head.
If it weren't for this war would they be dead...

For now however, my thoughts are on.
Midday dreaming of days back home.

54

Mispronounce the Hurt

When misery comes knocking at your door.
It isn't always clear what she's there for.

Sometimes even we haven't processed our thoughts.
Mispronouncing the hurt, each getting lost.

Within our own minds again.
Standing at the door frozen unable to call your friend.

Who's already there, sitting a few feet away.
As misery can come anytime of the day.

Her timings always met by a sway.
Changing the entire mood of the day.

The room becomes cold, as her black train sweeps the floor.
Here for an indefinite stay once more.

Unsure what she's even here for.
You mispronounce the hurt closing the door.

Which she left open, that frigid bitch.

Perhaps the world would be better off if I were lying in some ditch.

No that's her poison filling the air.
I can't even allow my mind to go there.

Searching deeply from within.
Finding the reason she's come once again.

Once mispronouncing the hurt.
You now know what to call it.

The reason she's come, the pain which she brought.
No longer able to feed on the toxins she sought.

Now that you know, she can finally go.
Free from your mind, you'll no longer find.

Her there absorbing your light.
You've won this battle, in the war on the night.

55

Miss Me? (Why Couldn't You See?)

Miss me? Why couldn't you see?
I was clearly drowning alone out to sea.
No life preserver found around me.

Steadily sinking further into the deep.
The thoughts of us my mind would keep.

Replaying over again.
Taking me back to when it began.

Tell me my darling, if I make it.
Giving you my heart, would you take it?

Could we consider starting again?
Being partners in war making a home we defend.

Together, once and for all.
Then I remember the crash, the fall.

Of our world as it came crumbling down.

Walking about that house, cold as ice.

Couldn't you see the light had left my eyes?
The soul that was within me had surely died.

Months of fighting defending our fort.
Who knew then the enemy was already within.

Blade ready to plunge into our back.
At the very moment they chose to attack.

Lying on the floor as a puddle formed.
I stand and stare as our relationship bled out.

With the knife still in your hand.
Dripping our memories both the good and bad.

Tell me, if you could go back.
Would you still betray me? A knife to the back.
Was it courage you seemed to lack?

To face me breaking the news.
It had been over long before then.
Fighting in vain no fort to defend.

It had already crumbled under the weight of your pen.
If you could rewrite the ending, would you write it that way
again?

Missing

If I became a prisoner of war.
Would the headlines read missing before.

It was too late.
Would this be what seals my fate?

Falling victim, a casualty of war.
Is that what I've been fighting for?

Just to lose, tell me who's going to take my place in the event I'm
gone.
If I were to go missing would you search the day long?

High and low.
Just how far would you be willing to go.

To find me, would you hold out hope?
In the event that I were missing, would you be able to cope?

My New Afternoons

Middle of the night, listening to the rain.
Sitting there thinking about this pain.

That had grown within me so.
I didn't know I could be my own foe.

It seems in life we can truly be.
Our own worst enemy.

Fighting battles only we know.
In the war on the night which doesn't show.

Sometimes those around.
Never realize our hearts on the ground.

Stomped on and in pieces, blood ran dry.
The three am hour is when I cry.

As the middle of the night has become my new afternoons.
Staying up to fight in the cover of darkness so that no one knows.
Story of life, I guess that's how it goes.

When you're facing a giant alone on your own.
There's no better feeling then making it back home.

If you're lucky enough to be on the winning side.
Buying time until the next, a moment you don't have to hide.

58

Not Now (Not Ever)

Soaring higher than the tallest pine.
This is it, you're losing your mind.

Unsure which planet that you're on.
Not knowing where to call home.

Walking around aimlessly, no where to go.
No money in your pocket, with nothing to show.

What do you do now?
You wonder, still chasing that high.

Tell me when did this become your desire?
Can you feel it? Walking through fire.

Always one step from losing it all.
Couldn't care less how far you'll fall.

Or who you take down with you as you go.
Is this what you want? Tell me so.

Why don't I just give up? You continually ask.

Waging War On The Night

It's not that easy considering your past.

I don't plan to give up, not now, not ever.
I meant it when I said it was you and I forever.

I'll be with you here, always by your side.
No matter how deep your soul tries to hide.

I'll be here waiting for that day.
The day you come home healed and whole.
This keeps me going, the hope in my soul.

59

Not the Only One On Your Mind

In a cafe down by the pier.
Unsure exactly how you ended up here.

Sitting watching the waves crash onto shore.
Secretly yearning to be with the one you've longed for.

So long, knowing you've had to be so strong while moving on.
You're with someone else now, your feelings could never show.

As they enter meeting you there.
Wishing to confess clearing the air.

Between you, putting it all on the table.
As they sat down you realized you weren't able.

To say the words aloud.
Sending their heart into a dark shroud.

However you've known what you would say.
In the event of this day.

You'd tell them they're not the only one on your mind.
That you once found something so hard to find.

That many never in their entire life even come close.
Despite their greatest efforts, battling past ghosts.

It was a storybook romance, a spring and summer you were swept away.
Taken to a place you still long for today.

Knowing this secret you've held so long.
So often sang in so many songs.

Was one they could never know.
Unable to imagine the day they would go.

Leaving you with just your shadow on the wall.
Behind you standing so tall.

Reaching the ceiling where you punched a hole.
You knew there was no way you'd ever let go.

So you kept your secret until the end.
Not telling a soul, not even your closest friend.

{ **60** }

Only Human

Faces in a crowd, screaming out loud.
Inaudible things, haunting your dreams.

Waking suddenly, sheets soaked.
Yet you're frozen from within to your skin.

Cold like a winters morning, alone in a vast empty field.
Snow crashing down around you using your blanket as a shield.

Keeping you alive, wondering why you can't cry.
If you did would it turn to ice?
Why can't the world be nice.

I'm only human, a soul in a shell.
Tell me God, why is this life hell?

Is this fair? Was I wicked?
Why is my life so damn twisted?

I'm only human, trapped in a cage.
Being tortured, taken out by rage.

Waging War On The Night

From who? I'll never know.
For now I wander, shivering through snow.

That surrounds even on a summers day.
Frozen like winter I stay.

Only human, so much I can bare.
Tell me, is there anyone out there?

Who can break these chains.
Bending the steel bars of this cage.

Finally free I would be.
If only someone could see...
I'm only human, I'm just me....

Open My Eyes

Open my eyes, let me see.
What I'm truly meant to be.

Open my eyes, show me what this wars really for.

Open my eyes, treat me right.
Show me how to stand up and fight.

In this battle, in this war.
Open my eyes, show me what it's all for.

Open my eyes, let me in.
I'm here willing to begin again.

Open my eyes, take me away.
To a place beyond the grave.

Open my eyes, let me be.
Everything I wanna be.

Open my eye, so that I might finally see.
Everything I needed, was always there within me.

Out of Touch

Phone ringing, someone at the door.
Kettle singing, mail pilling up on the floor.

Sitting in silence, ignoring the noise.
Staring at the note, this was your choice.

You've been out of touch for awhile.
Unable to be reached, a missing case file.

So many worry, yet you aren't even there.
Somewhere else, mind unaware.

Drafted to war, missing in action.
No longer taking part in your own faction.

No longer you pour from your cup into another.
Can't even be reached by your own mother.

Weeping in silence, out of touch with it all.
Tell me what lead you to give up and fall.

Down, facing the ground.

Allowing no one in, allowing no one around.

Weeping in silence as the war is lost.
Was it worth it, did you pay the cost?

Or was it your loved ones, which you left behind.
Did you consider them before making up your mind?

How I wish you hadn't, yet now you're at peace.
I'll love you forever, without cease.

Owning Your Scars

Returning from war, there's no moment more proud.
Then breaking through the fog, seeing past the dark shroud.

Which consumed every inch of your life.
Unable to see past it, causing much strife.

You made it this far, I knew that you could.
Owning your scars, as you should.

You made it through battle, coming out on the other side.
Finally being discharged, from the war on the night.

Pick Your Poison

Diving head first from the boat.
Quickly sinking afraid to float.

As the enemy is closing in.
Unable to breathe, unable to swim.

Just there existing, head underwater.
No where to go just sinking further.

Oxygen depleting, as darkness surrounds.
No thoughts of fleeing, no way out.

Pick your poison, which way to go.
By her army? No!

Mustn't think that way.
There has to be something, anything I can do.

Eyes bursting wider, using that last burst of everything left within
me.
Kicking off a piece of debris, full steaming ahead.

When the blast came, knocking me down a few feet.
Unable to hold my breath another moment.

I began rushing to the surface, breaking through the divide.
Between water and air, taking that life saving breath.

I see it, destruction all around.
Both my ship, and the nights were in pieces floating.

On top of the water some still on fire.
As ally forces jet over giving the all clear.

I see the rescue ship heading my way.
I use my absolute last ounce of strength.

To swim to a floating door from one of the two ships.
Where I was soon rescued from the nightmare I had just survived.

Looking back today if I had given up it would have been only
moments too soon.
Holding on to hope, and pushing the strength within myself to the
surface.

Came with a victory over the battle that nearly took me out.
No one's safe in the war on the night.

{ 65 }

Putting On Your Face

Painting on a smile, cheeks with no tears.
Noses not wrinkled, holding back fears.

Gown soaked in scarlet, from the wound in your chest.
Bleeding profusely, with each breath.

As you put on your face, creating the lie.
Which you'll use to hide, what's truly inside.

The feelings consuming, every inch.
Internally bruising, making you flinch.

Wincing in pain, yet playing it off.
Masking reality with a cough.

Asking for water you chug it down.
Hoping your feelings will thusly drown.

We paint on our best faces to go about our days.
Internally bleeding, our minds a maze.

Of barbwire and trenches, bombs bursting around.

As we do our best to defend our town.

From the enemy taking them down.
Waging war on the night, turning our hearts around.

66

Shades of Blue

Speeding down a mountain road.
The passing of colors, nothing owed.

Complete freedom, after all these years.
Finally free from all your fears.

No longer dreaming in shades of blue.
Your life now, a differing hue.

Out of the midnight, into gold.
Yours a story which must be told.

Your life was hard, harder than most.
Plagued by locusts, surrounded by ghost.

Constantly haunted by the sins of your past.
Yet now you're free at long last.

Breaking the chains, escaping the bars.
Driving down mountain roads, in classic cars.

Watching the colors change, as they pass by.

Waging War On The Night

Your life you've rearranged, gleam in your eye.

There's a glow about you now, replacing the shades of blue.
Your journey now is to show others they can do it too.

Breaking free from the chains, escaping the ghosts.
Being free to roam from coast to coast.

Snow Covered Paths

With any night comes a chill such as winter.
No matter the time or place, wind blowing, caressing your face.

Walking the streets of the city, or the paths of a small town.
The night doesn't take any of that into account.

When we come head on, with the night and her chill.
Crossing her snow covered paths, climbing her treacherous hills.

It doesn't matter, nothing is fair in war.
Isn't that what we're all here for?

Fighting in battle, waging war on the night.
Even through snow covered paths, we rise up and fight.

Sober (Letting Go Is Never Easy)

Three am, sitting on the floor.
Wondering what all this is for.

Dancing around lightning, switching from vice to vice.
Wondering how you even still have your life.

Knowing that being sober is where you need to be.
Knowing letting go is never easy.

Especially in the midst of war.
Wondering if the strength can come from within.

Finding out that it can.
Now knowing there's power in numbers.

Reaching out has helped you through.
Taking over the battle lines.

Planting your flag down firm.
Watching the enemy of the night squirm.

In defeat as you finally let go.
It was in you all along, your strength you learned to show.

{ **69** }

Songs That Get Us Through
(The Thick of It)

We all have them, we know what they are.
The songs that get us through the thick of it.

The songs that make us feel power coursing through our veins .
Chemicals rushing with each change .
Of the beat.

Songs with the power to curb even the strongest emotion.
Songs with the power to provoke emotion.

Songs to lift us, songs to bring us down .
Songs that get us through the hardest parts of life .

Songs that get us through the battles, in the war on the night.

Spending Our Last

We've all been there, spending our last.
Whether it's money, or energy to pass.

Through life's portals, from one day to the next.
The weight that it bares, a burden so heavy cutting deep into our
chest.

Whether we agree with it or not.
The way the world works is you either have it, or your don't.

There are times with plenty to spare.
Then there's times when you only have air.

Even now they charge for that.
There is truly no looking, nor turning back.

There's people out here living, and dying in the streets.
No bed to sleep on, nestled beneath sheets.

No table to sit at, no food to eat.
They're forced to bare the full brunt of the world.

Waging War On The Night

With those who have plenty looking down on their soul.
Judging them for what led them there, when that isn't our place.

What would you do if you were there?
In that place with nothing to spare.

Would you help them who have nothing to give.
Or would you hoard your wealth, not caring if they live...

We have to do better to become a world as one.
What if the downtrodden were your daughter, or son?

What would you think then?
As people walk on by while they have nothing to eat.

You'd too be crying out for help to make it through.
You don't know their story so who are you?

To judge, because they have less than you.
What a shame it is to have to see a world so gray.
Where we won't even help someone about to pass away.

For all those out there, please stay strong.
I love you, please fight for the right to your place in this world.

We're all human, we all bleed red.
Know you're not less than, and one day you will get ahead.

{ 71 }

Stay

You there with with the coat.
Tell me, can you drive a boat?

Off to the navy, come this way.
You're no longer free, you may no longer stay.

It isn't safe here, not while at war.
The nights army is approaching, that's what this drafts for.

We must go up in arms protecting our shore.
Their navy is strong, yet we've got more.

Hope on our side then they'll ever imagine.
What's waiting here for them, they can't begin to fathom.

The fight will be nasty, I won't lie.
We're planning to take them by both sea, and sky.

There will be soldiers here waiting to march from the ground.
To take on those who get past our team in the sound.

Many casualties are expected on both sides.

Waging War On The Night

In a war on the heart there's no place to hide.

Try as you may the nights poison is already here.
It's anywhere you look, no need to fear.

You've already been facing much of her wrath.
Now that you're with me you're on the path.

To wage war on the night, taking her head on.
Whether winning or losing great strength has been shown.

As so many fail to fight for themselves.
Letting their hearts go to battle.

Defended by none.
Shattered like glass, no light from the sun.

72

Still A Stranger

As the night faded into dawn.
You began to hear it, the radio was on.

A song was playing, you knew it well.
The bridge was slaying, that's when you fell.
Deep down the darkest well.

Into a memory, a time at war.
The night was the enemy you were fighting for.

Peace, at a time when nothing was calm.
You look into the mirror putting your armor on.

Yet the person looking back.
The memory of them you seem to lack.

As you're still a stranger to yourself.
Someone you must find.

Before you can win the war on the night.
Go find yourself, choose to fight.

Waging War On The Night

Without knowing who you truly are.
How can you know exactly what you're fighting for?

What do you value, your hopes? Your dreams?
In your mind you're seeking to know your life's themes.

Where you're going, what you want.
How to keep the night from being able to taunt.

You with something, leading you down a dark path.
One where you're forced to face her wrath.

You may be still a stranger to yourself.
Don't worry my darling, become who you dream.
Go out and create your own life's theme.

73

Strange Behavior

Looking over your shoulder, walking the path.
No ease in sight, no way to relax.

When you're at war no place is safe.
Yearning for more, wanting to leave this place.

Anxiety ridden, nerves on end.
Who can you trust? Can you have a friend?

When there are so many who end up betrayed.
It's a shame to think that's how it is these days.

Your closest friend can very well.
Be the one to push you, saying you fell.

On the tracks in front of the train.
Never to be heard from, or seen again.

Our greatest duty is too ourself.
Shielding our own hearts, fragile on a shelf.

So that maybe we can be sure no one can harm it unless we allow.

Waging War On The Night

Causing strange behavior, resulting in the raising of brows.

Wondering why you're acting this way.
When you feel no need to explain what would you say?
I'm saving my heartbreak for another day?

Sometimes it's the strange behavior that keeps us safe.
Each one unique with their own heart to hold.
Keeping it safe, that's true gold.

Survivors Of The Night

Four a.m. just before Dawn.
If you were back home the coffee would be on.

Yet you're in the midst of the war on the night.
Called up by your army, to rise up and fight.

Flying this plane, lower than you should.
Emergency landing, doing all that you could.

To save as many, including yourself.
Survivors of the night, until they open fire again.

For now we mend our gashes.
So that we may defend.

Against the next pawn.
Protecting our hearts to see another dawn.

Take It If You Can

Take it it's yours, giving up the fight.
You shout at Misery the mistress of the night.

Take it if you can.
Give it to your man.

My army and I will take this as a loss.
Spare him from this pain, take my heart in its place.
I'm strong enough to rise from the ashes time and time again.

Take it if you can.
You say taunting her all the while having a plan.

Knowing she couldn't resist.
You counter chaining her wrists.

To the tree, which she planned to hang him from.
Knowing that by morning the bitch would burn in the sun.

Barely escaping her grasp, you've earned a bit of rest.
Go now my dear, await your next test.

Take Me Higher

Take me higher, than the sky.
Take me higher, teach me to fly.

Take me higher, than I've ever gone.
Take me higher, than I've ever known.

Take me higher, to that place.
Take me higher, across the face.

Of the moon, and all her stars.
Take me higher, escaping these bars.

Take me higher, than the tallest trees.
Take me higher, help me flee.

Take me higher, to a better land.
Take me higher, here my hand.

Take me higher, where the pain will end.
Take me higher, come with me my friend.

Take me higher, where the war is fought.

Take me higher, where peace is sought.

{ 77 }

That Color Blue

Midnight, so bright.
Seeing into your soul that night.

Your name I never knew.
Only those eyes, that color blue.

Bluer than the ocean deep.
Bluer than the sky, the memories I'll keep.

Even in the midst of battle, there are cracks where hope falls.
That night you brought me back to life, during the war on the
night to beat it all.

{ **78** }

The Conversation (We Need To Be Having)

Despite the culture which you were born.
The conversation we need to be having doesn't come easy,
rather sharp as the prick of a thorn.

To the flesh, making bodies bleed.
This is a conversation we need to be having, an actual conversation indeed.

Many lives are lost who wage war on the night alone.
We need to ensure our best efforts to prevent more names being written in stone.

As a human we need another, that's just who we are.
Although for some uncomfortable, we have to reach down far.

Into our souls we have to let each other know.
That a good life is the goal.

A life that isn't lived alone.
A life which isn't misunderstood.

A life where no matter what you're facing, someone is always
there.
To catch you when you fall, to stop and help you stare.

At the stars, keeping them from bleeding.
A life which isn't lived any longer needing.

Someone who isn't there.
A life lost due to unfair.

Circumstances, a bad deal of the hand.
To know there's someone there who will rise with you and stand.

In the midst of the battle in the war on the night.
Standing beside you in your army ready to take arms and fight.

By your side all throughout the night.
Taking down her army ensuring another sight.

Of the sun rising over the hills behind your home.
Helping to keep your soul within you, helping you be strong.

When you're weak, that's what we're all here for.
To help one another achieve so much out of life and more.

That no matter what anyone is going through, there will always be
someone there.
Sometimes it's even a stranger, trust me that isn't rare.

Were sent into others lives, as others are sent into ours.
To help in ways unimaginable.

Waging War On The Night

As a human we're here to help another.
Even unrelated we're all sister and brother.

In the end it's all that matters, the soul which lies within.
Getting to the other side safely never alone again.

79

The Darkest Days

Standing in front of the mirror, refusing to look in.
Afraid there won't be anyone looking back again.

There's days when it's dark, the sun still in the sky.
These are the darkest days, the days you sit and cry.

For no reason other than wondering why you're still around.
Questioning if your purpose here will ever be found.

Or if you even have one.
Perhaps you were a mistake, all things one should never think.

Yet at a time we're all unable to deal with the pain.
A life which is constantly lived waging war on the night
standing in battle in the pouring rain.

With no army standing by your side.
The night able to find you, no matter where you hide.

There isn't anywhere safe as you face her alone.
Without the help of someone else, will you ever reach home?

Waging War On The Night

You wonder, that being a state of peace.
Will this war on the night rage on and never cease?

You wonder, hoping you make it through
one of the darkest days you've come to know.
Praying these feelings quickly go.

So that you can continue pressing on as you should.
There is a good life out there for you.

I promise it is out there.
Keep your eyes on the stars, shielding them from the glare.

Of the sun as it shines down on your face.
you've made it through to see another day.
Keep fighting you're worth it, remember these words I say.

80

The Heartbeat Of The Night

Wind blowing whispers through the trees.
Firefly's glowing near the leaves.

As the branches sway.
Bringing an end to another day.

The sky rippling with gentle magenta streaks.
Painted by hearts which seek.

The heartbeat of the night, reminding us we're alive.
Ready, and able to thrive.

Grabbing life by the horns.
Shielding our hearts from each roses thorns.

As we go about our days.
Feeling the heartbeat of the night, singing its praise.

In our minds,
as we continue to find.

Who we are,

with each gleam of every star.

In the sky above.
Can you feel it? My love.

The Hurt That Is Us

What is pain?
Did it lead you to emotional gain?

Did the fake smiles get you by?
Did you learn to fly, by the seat of your lies?

High above the trees.
Looking down judging me?

You see, the hurt that is us was the pattern of lies intertwined.
Into this world which I thought was mine.

When it never was, I was never a part.
Only ever a stepping stone used by you to take you higher.

Leaving me here on the ground.
Used, abused, fallen with no one around.

The hurt that is us, our story to tell.
A hurt I've come to know all too well.

The Lowest Point

Sinking deeper beneath the stone.
Now silent, the light had gone.

Within your eyes the colors had faded.
Forever your heart had become jaded.

Through misery, a battle lost.
Giving up the will, despite the cost.

Lives aren't always lost in death.
In the war on the night one cannot find rest.

The enemy invading, attacking from within.
No way to fight, no way to defend.

Lost all connection, no longer a friend.
Sheer isolation can cause a life to end.

Giving up in battle, allowing the darkness to consume.
Taking the light from every room.

Which you enter an instant chill.

The ambiance instantly killed.

Giving off energy, building a wall.
Around your heart three thousand feet tall.

No one can see over, nor do they try.
When you're at the lowest point on the other side.

Pushing away anyone who cares.
Rejecting their warmth, confirming their fears.

A battle lost in the war on the night.
Bringing winter in august, freezing time at midnight.

Until you seek within you, the will to find a reason to tear down
the wall.
No longer you'll hear anyone call.

{ 83 }

The Night From Within

Throwing your body onto a grenade.
Saving another from the mess you made.

Feeling the night as it began to invade.
The soul that is within you locked in that cage.

In war there isn't anyway out.
No matter condition, we're all in doubt.

Of our freedom, what's to come.
Has the night won, will we see the sun?

Rise in the eastern sky come morn.
Or will our hearts fall onto its thorn?

Piercing our souls clean through.
Bleeding out as the war ensues.

Lying there watching the enemy within.
A battle lost you're taken again.

Gashes mended, wounds dressed.

JACOB Z. WALDROUP

Your deepest secrets written on your chest.

For any, and all to read.
Your home stolen, no longer possessing the deed.

Locked in a cage, cast to the side.
The enemy within, your soul has died.

Once a monolith reduced and fried.
Locked in a cage taken by the other side.

A prisoner of war locked in your own fort.
The enemy raging within, no escape of any sort.

As the bars are wired.
Even to touch them would result in a fire.

Instantly consuming the shell which remains.
Causing both loss, and victory giving the night a gain.

Against you in the war which raged.
On the night from within your golden cage.

84

The Scars We Bare

We each have a story, ours to be told.
Written by the scars we bare.

Deep within our skin.
Allowing the outside a clear view in.

We each have a story, most we can't hide.
As the scars we bare lie on the outside.

Of our fortress, detailing the pain we've endured.
Some scars we bare bring a sickness unable to be cured.

You see in war, there's more than one cost.
Outlining multiple ways in which a battle can be lost.

Sometimes the arrow only grazes the skin.
Yet soaked in poison the damage was done.

Dying now slowly, time ticking away.
As the poison spreads, the night taking away.

What little time you had left, now unable to stay where you are.

Preparing your decent into the stars.
Your story now written deep in your skin as scars.

85

The Slow Burn

A lighter striking as you slowly inhale.
Smoke entering your lungs.

The rush of the chemicals entering your blood.
Indulging in the slow burn you've come to love.

All rational, and reason thrown into the wind.
Ignoring the damage, the burn you'll defend.

Against any, who try and make it make sense.
Your mind climbing walls, jumping that fence.

Running quickly to escape their concern.
Able to continue indulging in the slow burn.

Senses enthralled, a rush through your brain.
For mere moments no longer you feel pain.

Seeking that high, you'll never find again.
An endless journey, one you'll never win.

The feeling of lust, you've found for that vice.

JACOB Z. WALDROUP

Was created as a weapon by the night.

Knowing that causing a need for something they control.
The battles already lost, it was always their goal.

Nothings fair when it comes to war.
The need for that burn they were hoping for.

Gave them a win, yet you can't see the loss.
Until it's too late indebted to the enemy a cost.

You can't afford, handing you the weapon.
You've thrown yourself onto their sword.

86

The Way You Acted

It was never what you said, nor what you done.
It wasn't something you forgot, or that need to run.

Anytime anything got a little deep.
Unwilling to climb hills, let alone mountains steep.

Oh my darling, it was all in the way you acted.
That blacked out our sun.

When I brought you my fears.
Shutting down, refusing to hear.
What I was saying, or trying to at least.

Begging you to hear me, begging you to see.
Begging you to be with me beneath this sea.

In which I was drowning, no light breaking through.
No sight of the surface, so deep it was no longer blue.

Surrounded by darkness, unable to see.
Unable to hope, unable to dream.

You left me there, that's the reason why.
I've left you now, this is my final goodbye.

There Is Hope Out There (For All Of Us)

By the water sitting still.
Watching a seagull catching its prey.
The circle of life I watched today.

Flashing back, another life.
I was the prey dodging her knife.

Unsure I'd see another day.
Stranded alone in the midst of war.
Battle all around, frightened to my core.

I had this feeling, I was in her sight.
As I waged war on the night.

When In a flash, it happened that quick.
A sight which made me sick.

A woman before me, in a gown once white.
Now maroon had lost the fight.

Sacrificing herself, taking an arrow with my name.
Lying there wounded, I try and stop the bleeding.

With a heart heavy unable to understand.
I beg her to tell me why she threw herself on the nights blade.

Between heavy sighs,
as the blood dripped from the corner of her lips.

She tells me this. There's hope out there for us all.
Even through death we can't be afraid to fall.

When facing an enemy such as the night.
We have to spread our light.

From within.
It's the only way to fight, it's the only way to defend.

Another from her venom.
You my darling weren't meant to go today.
You still have a mission, a reason to stay.

With that she passed away in my arms.
Her words of wisdom, courage, and power.

Words I've taken with me that day on.
The war on the night for me was won..

88

There's No Way (We Lost Them)

As the archer takes aim.
With cannons loaded ready to exclaim.

Victory over the land, aflash in the night.
So bright no one could see.
Wiping out half of each sides army.

A scramble ensues, everyone trying to find their feet.
Unsure where the blast came, both armies retreat.

In the scuffle you're clearly in shock.
Seeing people wounded their world rocked.

You make it back observing the carnage.
That's when you realize your best friend,
who you swore to protect wasn't there.

Ignoring your own gashes.
You began searching, sifting through the ashes.

Hoping, praying there you'd find them alive.

That's when they told you to stop, they weren't there.
Instantly your heart would drop, nothing in war is fair.

Where an explosion within.
The night had taken your best friend.

In disbelief you say there's no way we lost them.
There's absolutely no way.

I was standing near them at the time of the blast.
How could I make it when they didn't?

Unable to comprehend.
I fell to my knees knowing the night had claimed this win.

Despite equal defeat.
In which each army had to retreat.

The night had won, taking away your sun.
The only thing left that kept you warm.

89

There's So Much More

Flakes of satin falling from the sky.
Temperatures plummet, stinging the eye.

Of all who try, and traverse.
In her dangerous conditions, through the nights universe.

Unable to see more than a few feet before you.
Unable to feel those who adore you.

The conditions of her winter deep within.
A punishment to the innocent lacking immense sin.

Her vail falling down on anyone who try.
Sinking deeper below her night sky.

When you come across a cabin.
Nestled deep in her woods.

Seeking refuge you begin to knock.
Yet the door opens before your hand,
can make contact with the wood.

JACOB Z. WALDROUP

A gentle lady with hair as white as the flakes,
which were falling down around you.
Smiling up, and welcoming you in.

Ushering you to a chair placed near the fire.
She gathered a blanket, and a cup of tea.

Where you began chatting, feeling you've know her all your days.
You began reciting your story, as if in a haze.

To this she replies, there's so much more out there if only you could
see.
There's paradise beyond the pain, this the spoils of victory.

Over the night, and her army.
Who's vail blacks out the sun.

Paradise lies beyond its edges.
Go now my child run!

She screams, as the cabin walls fall.
You run into the night dodging the explosions.

She had set a trap, yet it backfired on her.
By something she didn't expect.

Your guardian in the sky had met you there.
Taking you in, showing you care.

When you needed care the most.
She appeared before you as a gracious host.
At the time not knowing before you sat a ghost.

You learned from her how to break free.
Overcoming the night, and her army.

90

Three Months Ago

Three months ago, I felt the fall.
Three months ago, I lost it all.

Three months ago, is all it took.
Three months ago, my world was shook.

Three months ago, the pain that came.
Three months ago, you felt the same.

Three months ago, nothing was wrong.
Three months ago, my heart lost its song.

Three months ago, is when I'd lose.
The only thing worth anything to you.

Little did I know that you were only there.
To spend my checks, nails, and hair.

Three months ago, is when you'd leave.
Three months ago, I began to grieve.

Three months ago, I was a different person.

Waging War On The Night

Three months ago, you put a curse on.

My heart, body, & soul.
Three months ago, life took its toll.

Three months ago, is when they came.
Down from above prepared to arrange.

A last flight, for me back home.
Yet three months ago, they too were wrong.

Three months ago, I began to fight.
Three months ago, I took back my life.

Three months ago, a decision was made.
Changing my mind now would be insane.

Three months ago, I began to change.
Defeating the night, and her army surpassing the grave.

91

Tomorrow (Never Came)

Stumbling down the hall.
Onto the bed you fall.

Soon your child would enter your room.
Asking of you to warm up a meal.

Too late today.
I'll do it tomorrow you say.

Unbeknownst to you, the child hadn't eaten.
You weren't there, as you were down at the bar.

Never knowing the wiser.
You let your child starve.

The next morning you woke.
As you've done so many mornings before.
There you would find them, lying cold on the floor.

You see for that child, tomorrow never came.
Don't put off today what can't be changed.

Waging War On The Night

So many times they heard you say.
Tomorrow, in what ever way.

Until the day tomorrow never came.
Don't allow this to happen ever again.

92

Too Far Gone

How many times have you heard someone say.
They're too far gone to ever be saved...

How many times have they heard the same?
Why would they care to even try to change?

No one is ever too far gone.
As long as there is blood in their veins, and air in their lungs.

The choice is one they have to make.
Yet too far gone, always a mistake.

To assume that they are.
When all the while they're under fire.

Fighting a battle, waging war on the night.
Inside themselves is a sight.

That you probably couldn't begin to handle.

So don't you dare assume to know their vices.
Tell me are you willing to pay the prices?

That the toll of your ignorance cost.
Tell me, are willing to allow a life lost?

Their blood thusly stained upon your hands.
For the rest of your time here on this land.

No my darling, it doesn't wash off.
So don't you dare tell them they're too far gone.

Underneath The
Bleeding Stars

Lying in a trench, as the enemies fire rained down.
Ambushed, our base taken, seeking to not be found.

We flee to not be forsaken by the remaining soldiers.
Which now there were few as the shells continue to burst.

Looking into the sky I see maroon stars swimming in a scarlet sea.
There I lie underneath the bleeding stars.

Hoping to make it out alive, as another battle is lost.
As the enemy continues to drive out our side.

What's been lost cannot be found.
Lives untraceable their souls irreplaceable.

In this life their battle is over, their war was fought.
They gave their all, not intending to be caught.

In the dark all alone, robbed of the chance to ever see home again.
In the war on the night we failed to defend.

We Don't Do That Anymore

Today you find yourself in a place of peace and well-being.
Yet it hasn't always been that way, has it darling?

No? That's okay.
Because you made it here today.

Rising above as a colonel in your army.
Able to say we don't do that anymore.

The things that made us change.
The things that cost us prices to fuel our vices.

We don't do that anymore.
The things which cost us loved ones.

Friends, family, people you've always known.
Things which cost you time which cannot be undone.

Things that cost you power over your mind, body, & soul.
Things which fed the night bringing her closer to her goal.

Often wishing to break free from her chains.

Yet unable to say no when she taunted you,
with promises to end the pain.

Promises always empty, as the pain was never cured.
You finally made it to the day you've so longed for.

A new someone who can now see the sun as they go about their
days.
No longer cloaked in the nights veil, walking around in her haze.

When The Night Calls (And You're All Alone)

When the night calls, and you're all alone in the world.
With nothing, but the clock on the wall.

Ticking slowly as time continues to pass.
It's in these moments we look into the glass.

That is the mirror, which hangs on our walls.
Peering into our souls, as if it knows.

All of the secrets we try to keep.
The ghosts that haunt us, keeping us from sleep.

When the night calls, and you're all alone.
Is the time of day when it's hardest to get through.

As no one is there, it's just you.
With your thoughts, as you wait for a new day.

When the night calls, and you're all alone.
Never a better time to hang up the phone.

Never negotiate with the night.
She's a sly one, lusting for a fight.

When The Night Calls
(Anytime Of The Day)

When the night calls anytime of the day.
You have to be ready, no matter what she might say.

Her sweet alluring voice, as it whispers through the phone.
Intoxicating you with her poison, convincing you whatever isn't
wrong.
If you start resisting, she'll pull you back in with a song.

Overcoming your senses, as her venom slowly burns.
Deep within your veins, as your stomach turns.

She takes hold of the reigns, leading you away from battle.
The war is lost, tying you to her saddle.

Hauling you off, throwing you into her brig.
Leaving you there to smother, with no light or air.
When the night calls, leave her there...

{ 97 }

Why...? (Can't You See Me?)

Making your way down a crowded street.
Seeing the place you had agreed to meet.

Arriving early, not to be late.
You sit by the window, going over what you'd say.

Placing an order for coffee you remember still.

Gestures long unappreciated.
Your heart slowly becoming jaded.

You planned to ask in this quaint cafe.
Why? Can't you see me? Does it have to be this way?

All you've wanted for so long.
Is to be noticed for all you've done,
and that the sacrifices in which you've made.

Haven't been done so in vain.
Can they not see, they're causing you pain?

Yet each time you act as if everything is fine.

Waging War On The Night

When it isn't, today that ends.

If they can't appreciate you.
Perhaps you're just meant to be friends.

The hurt this has caused you, you'd yet to say.
Waging war on the night in silence.

With the bombs crashing down.
Not even a whimper, let alone a sound.

Today was the day you look the night in her eye.
Telling her to kiss your ass, as you say goodbye.

From that moment forward.
You chose to choose you.

Over anything else which fuels the night
Starving her hunger, smothering her on site.

Todays the day you plan to ask.
Why? Can you see me? They better act fast...

{ 98 }

Worn, Torn, Re-Born

As we wage war on the night, and her army.
There are phases which we go through.

The memories of what was, cause our hearts to be worn.
By the journey which brought us here.

The memories of the pain, cause our hearts to be torn.
As we remember the fear.

Then there's the memories of our victories, in many battles of this
war.
Causing our hearts to slowly be re-born.

War isn't won all at once.
There's many stages we each go through.

Unique experiences, battles of our own.
It's once we've fought them we realize we've grown.

Through trial comes strength.
Without the night we wouldn't appreciate the light.

You Could Have Asked (I Was Begging You To)

Waiting tables down at our place.
Though it's been ages since I saw your face.,

Hoping one day you might walk in.
Maybe we chat, begin again.

If I saw you, I know what I'd say.
I'd tell you something I've had on my mind for years.
One which has haunted me, causing me tears.

You could have asked me, I was begging you to...
Why did you leave me that color blue...

Ghosted, alone, on a silent ship in the night.
No will to stand up, no reason to fight.

No longer able to see the light.
I fought a dark battle waging war on the night.

In order to get myself back here.

JACOB Z. WALDROUP

Feeling somewhat alright.

So if you were to walk in here today.
I'd look you in the eye thusly, and say.

You could have asked me, I was begging you to.
Instead you left me in a world without hue.

Devoid of color, no light in the sky.
You left me here in the midst of battle alone to die.

You could have asked me, I was begging you to.
If only you'd asked me, I'd have told you.

What was on my mind.
Searching my heart together we'd find.

A reason to stay in the light.
If only you'd asked me, that bitter cold night.

You Didn't Know

Snow covering the window seal.
No light in the room, no credit left on the bill.

Only the flicker from the fire in its place.
Warming the room, illuminating your face.

Cabinets empty, well ran dry.
No longer you sit, and cry.

Doing all you could to stop it.
They only reached deeper into your pocket.

Taking more from you, than you had to give.
No way to keep up, no reason to live.

Yet you won't allow yourself to think it.
As you didn't know there were anyway out.
As your ship sank deeper into this bout.

Of depression you found yourself in.
So numb from it all, sails without wind.

JACOB Z. WALDROUP

Sitting without motion out from the shore.
Caressing the mist from the ocean as you ball up your fist.

Ready to get out, making things right.
Now you're ready to put up a fight.

You didn't know how bad it had gotten.
Until this moment you'd all but forgotten.

Now you can see just how bad.
Knowing it can't be, now you're just mad.

Finally confiding in another to help you fight.
To help you defend your home.

With the little that remain.
You will do what you can to strengthen every vein

That's left pumping blood into your life.
As you decide to wage war on the night.

About The Author

"Never mind about me
focus on the art
which I've created, and remember
no where in life
are we promised
a rose garden
without thorns."

J.

www.ingramcontent.com/pod-product-compliance
Lightning Source LLC
Chambersburg PA
CBHW010752150726
48196CB00008B/568